DEDICATIONS

This book is dedicated to my
wonderful and supportive wife Gillian.
Also to our two boys, Ruairidh and
Ciaran, who have started coming up
with jokes of their own so it seems that
this is hereditary. I love you all so
much and would be nowhere without
you.

Theo

Enjoy the book!

@IMgme

INTRODUCTION

When you ask someone 'would you like to hear a pun'? They will probably groan and say no. But if you ask someone if they would like to hear a joke, most would say yes. And invariably it ends up being a pun of some sort and they will laugh away. No wonder puns are so mispunderstood.

Paronomasia (thanks Wikipedia) is not a new thing. Puns have been used throughout history. They were used in ancient Egypt. The Mayans used them. The Romans did too. They are included in religious texts. Shakespeare and Lewis Carroll used them. We see them every day in advertising, on shop fronts, TV shows, in our newspapers. They say that in London you are never more than 6 feet away from a rat but I would suggest that you are never more than 3 feet away from a pun such is the ubiquity of them.

But you have people that would much rather come face to face with a rat than a pun. Why is that? Is it because they have been around for such a long time? Because they are everywhere in our lives? Because people don't find 'dad jokes' funny? There could be a multitude of reasons but I'm assuming none apply to you because you are reading this and this is, well, a book of puns. A book FULL of puns. All collated from my own strange little head and presented to you in this wonderful book that you're holding. Or tablet if it's an e-book. Or speaker if it's the audiobook version. Delete as appropriate. But only in your mind because 2 of the options would severely ruin your device if you physically did it with a pen.

You would think that I am writing to a word count here and trying to fill as much as I can with nonsense but that would not only be untrue but also wrong, erroneous, inaccurate, made up and flawed. Truth is, I can't write introductions. I can't write stories and observations. But I can write PUNS. One liners, dad jokes, wordplay, jokes- whatever you want to call them- that's what I do. And this introduction is honestly just a stream of consciousness that probably goes to show a little of how my mind works and how gibberish can just fall out of my head and onto a Google document (I would have said paper, or even Word document, but hey, it is 2022).

I have been writing puns for about 8 years now. At least actively writing them. I started doing stand up comedy in 2009 and always loved the material that I wrote. The problem was, the audiences didn't seem to share the same love that I had for my witty observations and quirks on human existence. But what I always had in my set were about 4 or 5 wordplay jokes. I only used them as I couldn't think of any decent segues between my other bits of material but that was the bit of my routine that got a consistency of laughter. For some reason, it only took me about 4 years to realise this but once I did, I embraced my new found love of puns.

Since then I have been writing pretty much every day and have participated in The UK Pun Championships, being a finalist in 4 of them, had hour long shows at many comedy festivals including Glasgow, Yorkshire and the Edinburgh Fringe, had material featured in various newspapers and radio shows and to cap it all, an appearance on Britain's Got Talent in 2022 at the London Palladium. Someone more bitter may suggest that I was no more than 6 feet away from rats that night but it was an experience that I treasure. There is also a show that I run called the UK Pun Off which has amassed hundreds of thousands of views on our Facebook and YouTube pages.

This is just a collection from the thousands of jokes that I have written over the past few years put into one handy collection. It is not possible to tell all of the jokes in one show or one video so having this to hand whenever the need for a good pun arises will stand you in good stead. It has been quite the task to select which ones to choose as some jokes only work well in my head, are better said than read and vice versa, are simply not funny, have been done before etc but I do hope that you enjoy it and a big thanks to Stevie Vegas (@SteveJuggler on the Twitter machine) for letting me know which ones those were.

Dedication

Introduction

CONTENTS

ANIMALS

If you are going to poke cattle with a guitar, you should make sure it's acoustic.

I had a pig as my servant. It was at my bacon call.

There was a mayonnaise, onion and cabbage mix that told the lions, gorillas and pandas what to do. It was the coleslaw of the jungle.

Bears are more popular than they used to be. It's an ursine of the times.

A cat took exception to me referencing it having its ovaries removed. But I call a spayed a spayed.

There was a lion that couldn't grow its hair although its vocal chords were fine. It never manes but it roars.

When a cat gets hurt, it makes a noise like me, ow.

Did you know that the most common place that you'll find young female horses in America is filly.

There was an alpha dog that made a lot of noise when he was at the pub. He was bar king.

There was an insect of great significance that was bought in from overseas. It was import ant.

My cat regurgitated this big clump of oregano. It was herbal.

My closest friend hit me over the head with a platter of pollen. I felt bee trayed.

I heard this cow singing and it really moooved me.

If I'm planning on seriously competing at this year's giant rabbit championship, I need to raise my game.

When James 1st was King of England, a heron-like bird put on a pantomime. It was Jacobean stork.

This male sheep was going on and on and on about how much jewelry it had. It was rambling.

My girlfriend had a spiny, spherical, hard shelled sea creature on top of her head. But never mind that, you should sea urchin.

My baby goat had 2 bean shaped organs half way down its legs. They were its kidneys.

I asked a South African farmer what kind of birds he kept. He said "geese". I said, "I dunno, is it chickens?"

A dog dressed up as a cat for a photo shoot. It just wasn't fit for pur pose.

A spider has taken a chunk out of itself whilst climbing up the water spout. It was an incy dent.

When bears start to go into a resting state around autumn, they like to set fire to bits of wood to keep themselves warm. The ones that are low on the ground don't need much so they'll set fire to about four or five bits but the high burn eight.

I've got a nocturnal animal that I put my jaw in every night to cool it down. It's my chinchilla.

A friend of mine told me to go and ask a gorilla what family order he belonged to. I replied 'I don't like to pry mate'.

I used to go and see my collection of birds quite regularly. Now I just go aviary once in a while.

There was this wild dog that could do the jobs of Wolves, Coyotes and Hyenas. He was a jackal of all trades.

I know someone that is really frightened of small dogs. Oh, he is terrierfied.

I let all of my birds fly south in the winter whilst dropping parmesan and mozzarella from the sky. They we migrating geese.

The mood in my house changed when I found out that my kitten was scared of green clumpy plants. It was quite the cat moss fear.

There was a group of fish wearing turbans all trying desperately to grab hold of something. They were sikh reachers.

If a pig got stuck in a bush, would it become a hedgehog?

A fish wanted me to send it a well known saying via twitter. Carpe diem.

You know that there's a revelation about moths that has recently come to light.

Training male deer to race is a good way to make a fast buck.

SPORT & LEISURE

Maradona couldn't identify a huge white bird with a long beak and large throat pouch. But, don't worry, pelican.

What did the referee say to the fat boxer to let him know more food had just arrived? Seconds out, round one.

I was really honoured when I found a swiss tennis player in my hat. It was a real Federer in my cap.

Jeff Goldblum loves rugby. But he doesn't know which part of his brain to use when talking about it. He should use the fly half.

Have you heard that the architect of barcelonas stadium used to be very butch and macho? Yeah, but he's camp nou.

There was a rough Mexican central defender. He was particularly tough in the taco.

Swimming pool lifeguards. They need to be deep end able.

My wife has to use the bumpers when bowling cos if it went off the lane, it would really gutter.

At the fruit football match, when the lemon got injured, the astute manager's tactics were too sublime.

To avoid injuries, you should use the opportunity to train boxers sparringly.

Some Swedish tennis players come into this world born human, some born machine and some Bjorn Borg.

There was a golfer with a lisp that disproved the misconception that he always landed in the sandy area of the golf course. He was a myth debunker.

I got drunk on little bottles of whiskey and rum whilst playing pitch and putt. It was miniature golf.

When I'm in my car, I use this huge golf club to get the creases out of my clothes. It's my driving iron.

Stephen Hendry would try and leave very discreetly with his wife after his matches. He always snooker out of there.

I never use contactless when i pay for bowling, i always enter my pin.

A female boxer demanded more money to showcase her best punch. She wanted to uppercut.

What dance do they do on ice rinks? The ice hockey cokey.

There was a great player that had the upper body of a human and the lower half of a horse. He was a centaur forward.

I know that a lot of people's favourite Cameroonian footballer to model shoes has been Roger Milla. But for me it's still Eto'o.

Did you know that the world sit-up champion is a yeti? He's known as the abdominal snowman.

I was giving a friend of mine a massage when they became really irritable. I must have rubbed them up the wrong way.

If someone organised a trampoline festival, would they need a lot of bouncers?

I'd always sweat hot chilli sauce during workouts. It was peri perispiration.

John McEnroe can't believe the Italian top flight is as good as it is. You can often hear him scream 'you cannot be Serie a'.

What is a frog's favourite game?

Croakey.

Bodybuilders are all very keen scientists. They love their physiques.

Some people think that Carl Lewis is America's greatest Olympian because he rents his house but Jesse Owens.

Britain's most successful track athlete has turned to staying in his room all the time, listening to depressing music and wearing dark clothes. It's Emo Farrah.

A lot of boxers think about their hair during fights. Sometimes they think they'd like it short but then also consider hair extensions. They don't know whether to bob or weave.

SPOONERISMS

You want to know how to iron jeans?
Let me denim straight.

There was a plumber working away
with a bracelet of Orion's belt on his
wrist whilst singing the American
national anthem. He was the star
bangled spanner.

I became quite angry when I got found out for shouting. I got caught under the holler.

I had a friend that got really angry when he would light up a wicker container. He would completely glow a basket.

Bucks Fizz won Eurovision with their song about remembering to apply the right amount of foundation, lipstick and blusher. Minding your make up.

There was an insect that ate so much that it made his father die. It was the very hungry pater killer.

Have you heard about the famous martial arts actor that was in fact a poorly made french cheese? Loose Brie.

There was this really spotty snooker player that I couldn't take my eyes off of but he was absolutely rubbish. A watched boil never pots.

Donkeys are so careless with their jokes. A mule and his funny are easily parted.

I was in a rush to drive to an event in which I had to combine flowers into an award that I was giving. I just put the petal to the medal.

Peter Capaldi's character in The Thick of It was always messing about with an absorbent powder. He was a talcum mucker.

ENTERTAINMENT

Noel Gallacher was asked if he knew why everyone kept referring to Liam as a flower. He said "what, you mean orchid?".

Zippy and George have paid the rent on their single levelled cottage but bungalows.

I sang a Christmas song out in the street about a big cat woman that fed her husband to a tiger. I was carol buskin'.

I love Ghostbusters. Winston Zeddermore, Ray Stanz, Peter Venkman and eh, thingy Spengler. Can't believe that I forgot his name. I really have Egon my face.

Do you know how Mr T counts? He uses a B A Barabacus.

I got into trouble for taking a bath in The Da Vinci Code, 50 Shades of Grey and Twilight. I really was in the bad books.

When rappers need to go travelling, they need Tupac.

Victoria Beckham doesn't need to read sworn testimonies to know the truth. She just hears it affidavit.

The sci fi film about Tom Cruise compiling an account of under 16's drinking hot beverages. the minor tea report.

There's a bird that can sing House of the Rising Sun and Stairway to Heaven. It's A minor bird.

How do you know Po is the most intelligent Teletubby? Cos she is well red.

Someone once criticised my playing of the squeezebox but I said, "yeah, that's accordion to you...".

Someone said that I wasn't able to play a smaller version of the harp but they're a lyre.

Have you heard of the Indonesian Rat Pack tribute act? Its led by Frank Sumatra.

Who is the best singer at floating? Buoyancy.

A PR guy was showing gratitude to concert goers after George Michael teamed up with a chav. He was the Wham, bam, thank you man.

My girlfriend bought a fake snake from the lead singer of the Eurythmics. It seems that Annie conned her.

When I wash the dishes, I love to dance. My feet are all over the place but at least my hands are in sink.

I once spotted this X-factor runner up in Madagascar with some really cute monkey-like creatures. I thought "Awww Lemurs!".

I used to have a problem constantly listing 1970s rock anthems but I'm all right now.

Superman's nemesis is an intricate and obscure individual. He is a complex Luthor.

There is a new superhero that makes people scratch at their heads. He's brilliant! In fact, he's Marvel louse.

I was asked to castrate cats. Well I thought Mr Mistofolees and old Deuteronomy were terrible but Grizabella was fabulous.

When Blondie split up, as they were a rock group, the lead singer should have changed her name to Debris Harry.

The person that plays Bumblebee in the transformer films. He's quite the character.

How did Belle get to the small restaurant across the lake? The bistro? Well he could hardly make her swim.

Elton John wrote a song about his addiction to artificial sweetener. "And it's my saccharine vice".

I was in charge of a forum for judging vespa bikes, The Jam cover bands and fighting with rockers. I was the mod rater.

I've always found shows like Little Britain and The Fast Show a bit, well, sketchy.

There was a guy that kidnapped Pennywise and the police never knew. He got away with It.

I was telling these really inappropriate jokes to Bruce Willis. I've got a sixth sense of humour.

Groot was so frustrated that his raccoon pal couldn't understand that paintings weren't part of quantum physics. It's not science, rocket.

What's a turtle's favourite past time? Terrapin bowling.

Captain Hook. He knows question marks like the back of his hand.

What is Thor's favourite festival?
Valhallowe'en.

I keep on pulling these community chest cards in Monopoly. Huh, chance would be a fine thing.

Sean Connery went to a pebbled beach and asked 'is this a shingle beach?' I replied, 'no, there are married couples here, too'.

Rod Stewart wanted to travel to a fictional Yorkshire country estate in the early 20th Century. To get there he had to take the Downton Train.

A country music star had a toy that committed a heinous crime but wanted her to be released from prison. She wanted her dolly pardoned.

When you need a country music star in a hurry and have no time to make a costume, you have to call a tailor, swift.

There was a film that featured just a big jug of beer and it won an Oscar. It was for best pitcher. I think it featured Alec Guinness and Jodie Fosters.

Did you hear about the gorilla martial arts master? King Kung Fu.

A group of gorillas found a feral boy on the beach covered in a black sticky substance and decided to raise him as their own. They named him tar sand.

A 70's medical examiner was trying to identify a snow shelter. It was quinzee

.

The little white robot from Star Wars has mastered taking alternate routes of travel. He has the art to detour.

I hear Marshall Mathers is going into the colonic irrigation business. He'll now be known as Eminenima.

There was this huge animal with a trunk, tusks and big ears that was obsessed with a young Parisian soprano. It was the elephantom of the opera.

What about that opera where Sylvester Stallone presents a big jug of beer that cost just more than 99 cents? The Rocky Dollar Pitcher Show.

There is a small, hard bodied bug that wrote many Broadway musicals. PG Woodlouse.

There was a musical about a French chicken that transforms into a man when it puts big shoes on. Poussin boots.

There was someone going to Hawaii to give an award to a Scottish singer. They're going to honour Lulu.

At the fictional gangster football match, Cillian Murphy played a blinder.

When Ebenezer Scrooge was asked where the Beatles were discovered, he said 'bar Hamburg'.

I was watching Ghostbusters on Netflix and Dailymotion at the same time and a total protonic reversal happened. I should have known never to cross the streams.

The ringmaster is constantly looking for homemade cigarettes. He's always requesting a "roll up roll up".

Have you heard about the Scottish superhero with a bow and arrow? Hawkeye.

Garrett Hedlund said goodbye to Jeff Bridges as he became a collapsing supernova. That's because he is the neutron star.

The likes of Ice T and Grandmaster Flash no longer want to be called rappers. At their age, it's more about the hip op.

A lot of kids' movies are shown for a very cheap price at a certain cinema. It's the nickel Odeon.

Windsor Davies and Donald Sinden were fans of most of the authors of the late 19th century but never the Twain.

Glen Campbell wrote a country song about an underweight gunslinger. He was the nine stone cowboy.

Luke Skywalker went to Saudi Arabia and was made a Sir. He was a Jeddah knight.

The author of Animal Farm might have been sick when he wrote his books. Orwell.

My favourite films are the ones about decaying and rotting meat. The carrion films.

I kidnapped the That's Life presenter and wouldn't give her back until Jesus rose from the dead. It was my Easter ransom.

You'll never guess what Harry Potter did when he couldn't think of the vessel to use to mix up a magic potion. Cauldron? No, he gave Hermione a text I think.

Some west coast hip hop artists customised their cars to be made of salt. It was their sodium chlorider.

Roald Dahl wrote about this huge big statue of a honey making insect. It was a bee effigy.

When I was Cinderella, I got so annoyed by my cast mates bullying the guy that played my servant. They were really pushing my Buttons.

PAST & PRESENT (HISTORY AND TECHNOLOGY)

Did you hear about the archaeologists' party where they were looking for lower leg remains? It was a shindig.

I don't like Internet Explorer or Firefox. I think they don't work well because they feel a bit rushed as browsers. So I much prefer to use the Google one. That's because Chrome wasn't built in a day.

When Perseus went to kill Medusa he was really confident. He knew it was a Gorgon conclusion.

I travelled from Dover to Calais, riding on a remote control. I was channel surfing.

Have you heard about the excited history book? It was full of beens.

You know the guy that crucified Jesus? He was doing a kind of yoga whilst he did it. It was Pontius Pilates.

There was a mass exodus in the catering industry in Egypt. Folk were told to take everything but the kitchen Sphinx.

Who is it that is singing those religious songs? Hymn?

Has anyone ever thought about where the word etymology comes from?

When God cast the plagues on Egypt, he never thought about how expensive it would be. That's why, by the time he got to number 8, it was locust.

The name of a 10 year period had actually shortened from 11 because it decade.

I hate that I get Facebook ads for funky dancing ex US vice presidents. I blame the dodgy Al Gore rhythms.

I must admit, I used to go onto Facebook just to troll people but I'd only do it from my bathroom. I was finally caught when they traced my IP address.

The big problem facing lumberjacks that can't access their computers is that they can't get past the login screen.

There was this guy that went around digging up old bottles of cider and super lager. He was an alkyologist.

I wanted to find out what the noise my baby was making so I had to google "gaga".

There was this really funny film about the Battle of Hastings. It was absolutely historical.

If you were at a computerised hive and you tried to control B, that would be a bold move.

When my internet connection got shut down, it turned into my RIP address.

I saved all my files onto a USB and someone stole it. They really got my back up.

Which US president would win a war in outer space? Ronald ray gun.

All these stories about Saint George, they tend to drag-on.

You know the name of the guy that invented the spear used in cavalry charges? Lance.

I decided against posting an inspirational quote alongside a picture on twitter. It was a bit meme spirited.

When the inventor of the ZIP file, Phillip Katz, died, he was encrypted.

An Egyptian pharaoh said he saw a sheep. Ramesses? No, it was definitely a sheep.

When the goddess of harvest and agriculture came to town, i just had Demeter.

I went to Jordan to visit a near 2 and a half thousand year old site but I was really scared. In fact, i was Petrafied.

There's this great picture online of the 16th US president inviting a sandwich cookie to an employment social media site. It's the linkdin meme oreo.

People always go on and on about their hanging gardens. They just Babylon. Nowadays Iraq it up to experience.

I keep on pressing F1 on my computer. It's become a habit. I need help.

The condiment that the titans used in ancient Greece was tartarus sauce.

The English scientific philosopher that was best known for being a shining light in Paris was Frances Beacon.

The American civil rights campaigner that was the boss of a bath sponge was Martin Loofah King.

My wife and I were in competition to come up with a high speed electron. I beta.

My favourite French philosopher named after a hostess trolley is Rene Teacart.

If someone is loading up an ancient Korean multiple missile firing weapon, you need to hwacha self.

I checked the weather forecast and I think it said that emails should expect rain. No, wait, it said the Outlook was cloudy.

Have you heard about the new Jesus crisps? They're quite savioury.

SCIENCE AND HEALTH

I like to change the colour of fast growing herbs in my garden. Oh sorry, I dye cress...

I share a car when going to work but my wrists get really numb and tingly whenever we go through an underpass. It's car pool tunnel syndrome.

I can't understand how people can be lactose intolerant. I mean, some of these people may have lost them due to frostbite or something.

I wasn't sure whether to go to the party with my liver or my spleen. In the end, I just went with my gut.

I asked a friend if my breath smelled of fish. I waited for their answer with baited breath.

I bet your university doesn't teach about mushrooms. But mycologies do.

Quite often, when I go out in the rain, I will find myself a bit damp. Not all the time but moist of the time.

If you are selfish and need stitches, you need to suture self.

Someone dropped a subway sandwich in the ocean. It ended up in the marinara trench.

Someone was on trial for wagering £500 that he could apply a bandage. He was done for aiding and abetting.

There was a huge, jacked up rock flying about outer space. It was a-steroid. But that's a huge assumption to say it was on steroids. It might just have been a big metetor.

One of the great questions in physics is how to destroy anti-matter. It's easy. With uncle father.

There is a flat piece of land with no trees or buildings that has consistent downpours. It is open terrain.

I moved out of the biggest city in Austria to the second biggest city because of pollution. Turns out that the Graz is greener.

If you have back problems when visiting Egypt, you should visit a Cairopractor.

People that only use their mobiles for eBay, is that their sell phone?

We wanted to name our dog after a unit of time but we took so long in deciding, we eventually had to call it a day.

I could talk about asphyxiation until I'm blue in the face.

I've got loads of photos of egg whites. I keep them in a photo albumen.

My mother's sister always gets up before noon. She's my ante meridian.

It's alright to grow fungus in a tight space 'cos you don't need mushroom.

A friend told me they couldn't operate automatic doors. I said, 'let me walk you through it'.

What two kinds of watches does a lumberjack use? Digital analog.

To cure claustrophobia, you really need to think outside the box.

The amount of times I've tried to change a plug unsuccessfully. It's shocking.

I am determined to get inside an abcess. In fact, I incyst.

I had these bony vegetables at the side of my feet. They were bunions.

Which is the most phlegmy country? Qatar.

There are so many people passing judgement on ice these days. It's so frostrating.

The sponge just loved to wet itself over and over again. It was so self absorbed.

My sister wanted a potion for eternal life but my divine, lizard brother said that he could help out. I recommended elixir.

I went out with this girl that had a nail infection. She was a fun gal.

Why were the red heads not allowed out in the sun? cos they auburn.

There was a guy that invented hearing aids made of meat filled pastries. He was a pioneer.

I made a joke about someone eating and drinking. It was just ingest.

I found out that my class for prolonged life was a success, everyone saw my pupils dilate.

My father had a sex change and now she is completely see through. She is my transparent.

If someone could tell me how to avoid hair loss, alopeciate it.

A vampire drained me and wanted to make tea. It makes my blood boil.

Instead of wearing leather boots, my vegan friend made her own by using loads of little nuts and saved a load of money. They were cash shoes.

If Torvill and Dean had psychological problems, would they go and see an ice shrink?

I wanted to print out an article about being able to regulate my bladder. I found it ironic that I had to press control p.

The fallopian tube is very protective of the eggs it transports to the uterus. Although you could say it was ovary protective.

How do you know that all weather forecasters are carnivores? They are all meat-etorologists.

I've been hoping to get a bit of heavy but short term rain. I've been assured it'll c'mon soon.

There were these two very well to do women who would meet socially around midday to go to the gym. They were ladies who lunge.

I was addicted to buying plants but I have given up. In fact, since 2015, I haven't botany.

I signed up so that, should I die, my remains go to my local kebab house. It's my donner card.

The king of the dinosaurs had a cravat that was in pain but still managed to complete the marathon. The tie ran a sore race.

Have you heard about the Mexican bodybuilder who ran out of protein shakes? No whey Jose.

One of the symptoms of Covid is continuously getting served Turkish meatballs. A persistent kofte.

My electrician brother recently had a sex change. Now she is my trans sister.

What's a Mexican's favourite skin care product? Oil of Olay.

Can you believe that there was a clown that refused to put on his face paint? Honestly, you couldn't make it up.

There is a doctor that treated skin conditions of elephants. He was a pachy dermatologist.

They say an apple a day keeps the doctor away. Well I've been drinking copious amounts of cider each day for years now and, if anything, my A&E visits have increased.

A couple of raisins took it in turns to reverse the direction of electricity. It was the alternating currant.

I've got a friend that had a bad experience taking suppositories. He said it rectum.

There was a lot of controversy about what should be aboard the craft that would send the first living thing into space. But, it was a dog, Laika or not.

I was recommended by a few people to go and ask a gentleman about why trees lose their leaves in autumn. When he asked why i approached him I said "deciduous the expert".

All astronauts are equipped against potential outbreaks of Covid in outer space as their spaceships have plenty of boosters.

You know the phrase about the large predatory lizards where one is visually overweight and the other just is greedy? Celluliter alligator, inner whale crocodile.

I was told that by the time that I showed symptoms of the virus, I actually had a large Peruvian empire in my system for some time. It was the inca bation period.

I was so frustrated with the state of the machine that was helping me breathe. I didn't complain at the time but I'd vent it later.

There was a letter in the middle of the alphabet that was singing the names of all the other letters. It was enchanting.

I was congratulated on the amount of times I successfully completed surgery on bones in the lower arm. But to be honest, it was ulna days work.

How do you know that seaweed, plankton and sea lettuce are homosexual? Cos they're algae.

I never understood Scrappy doo's catchphrase about the heavy rock singers molecule obsession. Lemme atom, lemme atom.

Ah, a cure for my red, itchy, blotchy skin. What a sight for psoriasis.

WORK

My dad was a pig rustler. That's how he brought home the bacon.

The lady in my local kebab shop is pregnant. Soon she will be hearing the pitta patter of tiny feet. I think her name is Donna.

I volunteered for the task of being a train but it seems that I bit off more than I could choo choo.

There was a murder in a jewellers and the victims were twins that worked there. They were dead ringers.

I recently lost my job at the clothing manufacturers where my job was to make final inspections on all the shirts. It was because I crossed my eyes and dotted the T's.

I worked at a dating agency for letters of the alphabet. It was the only job I could get at the time. I was just trying to make n's meet.

Popeye asked his customers how he could improve his business and they said that his girlfriend's shop was too small. To appease them, he had to extend the Olive branch.

I wasn't sure about the priest's idea to dress up for his sermon. Turned out to be a blessing in disguise.

The former Ugandan president loved paperwork. It was Idi Admin.

There was an entrepreneur that made his money swapping his stock in tomato sauces to biscuits. It's a real ragu's to rich teas story.

The mafia boss used a mule to access his office. It was his donkey.

I asked the pencil, ruler and stapler why they were standing so still. They said it was because they were stationary.

Have you heard that miners were given toothpaste every time they entered their work? They got it at the colgate.

I worked at the blackjack table in a casino when I had my hands chopped off. You wouldn't believe what I had to deal with.

I went into the Pandora shop and was sold a sausage and a notebook before I was given a bracelet. Well, third time's a charm.

I tried to get the accounts department to move their financial projections but they refused to budget.

The person in charge of the museum was giving marks out of 10 to all the people who were waiting to get in. He was the curator.

I recently got a job castrating animals, I had to say that I was still neuter it all.

The Jacuzzi repair man excelled at his job but for him it was sauna days work.

Why do all wine waiters stink? Cos they're sommelier.

My timid friend Catherine owned a sandwich shop. I called her deli cate.

Selling face creams is a difficult business so, when presented with them, you need to make the moisture opportunities.

2 composers were arguing about how to make a piece of work calmer. They had a score to settle.

Our chairman was going to give a presentation on yawning and being fatigued. It took place in the bored room.

It slipped my mind that I was responsible for compiling the guest list to the meeting of the clergy. I forgot to properly administer.

The 5 pence got refused entry into the police school because it wasn't copper material.

Trawlermen get paid in fish guts which is their gross pay but ironically whatever they catch with their line is their net.

I got offered a job as a frog. It was quite the hoppertunity.

Learning how to play small drums with my hands is a bongoing process.

I can see myself working at Kwik Fit for a long time. I think I'll be retiring there.

Have you heard about the sad greengrocer? He was melancholy.

There was a country full of stags so I felt that I had to make a donation.

Someone who will only trade in trout and haddock seem selfish to me.

I showed my willingness to be a part of the team of cheese shredders. I was integrating.

I was the model for a prosthetics company and I just started a new job at the very same factory that they were made! I'm still finding my feet.

A sailor went to CCC but couldn't because everyone else was blind copied into the email.

I've got a tractor that's solely used to collect my honey. It's only to get from hay to bee.

When I was told that I was going to have to produce yet another steel fastener for a hinge, I made a bolt for it.

I saw an advert looking for a chef that conservatively uses herbs. It asked for no thyme wasters.

A hypnotist said he was going to make his subject think they were experiencing life before they were born. He said 'and 3,2,1- you're back in the womb'.

A few years ago, the IRS was investigating Steve Jobs but he kept telling them facts about cakes. All they wanted to know was the Apple turnover.

I was teaching an uppercase typing class outside when it started to rain. So I told them to put caps on.

A high ranking police detective was always doing little odd jobs around the station. Everyone asked D.I, Y?

Cremating bodies. Quite the way to urn a living.

Northern wasps don't go to auction houses but southern bees do.

There was a pub that was sold at auction for a really cheap price. For the buyer, it was a bar gain.

Despite the seller insisting that the silk sofa was brand new, it looked satin to me.

GEOGRAPHY

I was trying to convince my friend to go to central Africa with me but he was really not up for it. Eventually, he Cameroon to the idea.

So, what was it you did to the button to gain access to the North Wales seaside town? I just Prestatyn.

My friend thought that a young frog was a bit German, I thought it was a tad pole myself.

The capital of China isn't as colourful as it used to be. It's Beijing.

Do you know that Southern Pacific islanders don't start their alphabet from 'a'? They start it Fiji

I went to a country in East Africa. Uganda? Well, I had a little look about.

I went to a fancy dress party in the former Soviet Union. Ukraine? Well, I was a digger actually but that was a good guess.

As soon as you go to Turkey, you get rewarded with a male cow. You get an instant bull.

I love going to the Vietnam capital to wind folk up. I just do it to Hanoi.

I'm going to get a property in the United Arab Emirates. Dubai? No, I think I'll rent at first.

A tiger climbed up a Scottish mountain. It was Ben gal.

In West Africa, my da stood up but Mali.

How do sheep put up shelves in the Caribbean? With Bah Hammers.

You are not allowed to wait in line for cigars in the biggest of the Caribbean island due to the Cuban.

Whenever I go to Boston, my dog likes to gather up treats from all around the state. We end up with a mass of chew sticks.

Loads of spiders in the Middle East. That's what arachnids.

Off the east coast of Africa, they drive electric cars but when I went over they were furious. In fact they were mad, a gas car!

I was due to walk barefoot across Antarctica, but I ended up getting cold feet.

Every time I entered a laundry raffle in Manitoba, I'd Winnipeg.

When I go mountain climbing in northern Spain, I am fixated at looking at peoples legs. All I see are a Pyrenees.

Have you heard about the jacked up Inca Pokemon? Macho Pikachu.

I had 2 kids back in ancient Rome, but I was estranged from their mother. She would never let me just pop round for a visit insisting that beforehand I had to Colosseum.

In Nepal, there are men that dress as dogs but never visit the capital. But the Kathmandu.

I like Romania when I need a nice relaxing holiday, I go to Bucharest.

There was a mixed breed cat in the Somalian capital that had some mental health problems. The Moghadishus.

There was a Mexican running around looking agitated and frantic. Wasn't my problem though. Hispanic.

Australian natives claim that they wrote 'Waterloo', 'Winner takes it all' and 'Mama mia'. They say they are Abbaoriginal.

The heaviest food in the world is from China. It's won ton.

If a horse was familiar with me in Zimbabwe, I'd expect it could be Rhodesia.

Do you know which parts of my body become painful by getting a covering over my teeth when I am visiting a former Yugoslav state? Baws, knee and hurts to go veneer.

FOOD AND DRINK

My wife has left me because of my pasta touching fetish. I'm feeling Cannelloni right now.

There was an artist that whenever he drew his subjects, he made them look like funny orange vegetables. He was a carrot caturist.

When someone asked me why I had a huge frozen chip as a walking stick, I told them it was McCain.

I went to a restaurant and ordered a filet mignon. Imagine my surprise when I was touched up by a small, one eyed yellow creature shouting 'banana'.

I'm collecting a load of meat from this older lamb. Hogget? No, i think i'll give it out quite equally actually.

When I was out to dinner in Spain, everyone ordered huge meals. When they offered me one, I had tapas.

I love spicy food. But I can't handle it when it lands on the back of my foot. It's my a chilles heel.

This guy was telling me how to make guacamole but I insisted that cucumber was the main ingredient. I was playing devil's avocado.

I was congratulated for slow cooking beef atop a mountain. High braise indeed.

I had to explain how to make tea without swearing. They were PG Tips.

The Oregano was all flattering and smarmy with the Garam Masala. It was trying to curry favour with the curry flavour.

I like waffles, lorne sausages, toast followed by 2 apple strudels side by side. That's a good square meal.

The Yorkshire police went to arrest this little orange fruit. It refused to kum quatley.

This little orange fruit was trying to force the other fruit out of the fruit bowl by pushing and slapping them. It was a satsumo.

My mate wouldn't give me any of his garlic mayonnaise so I appealed to him 'aioli want a little taste'.

My 2nd personality sacrificed an omelette in church. It was my altar eggo.

What is a genie's favourite drink?
Djinn.

I recently had a tragedy with some steak tartare but I don't want to talk about it. It's still a bit raw.

In my opinion, adding chocolate to coffee just makes a mochary out of it.

This bison tried to sell me some knock off brandy. It was a cognac.

The winner of the pancake making competition was so close, only a toss up could decide the winner.

A group of nursery school pupils planted some chocolate eggs with toys in them. It was a kindergarden.

Did you know that French fries weren't originally cooked in France? They were cooked in Greece.

My mate loves drinking beer when he is doing martial arts. He is known as high knee ken.

I was served this Turkish starter but all of the olives, cheeses and pickles were just strewn across the plate. It was so meze.

Our teacher asked if anyone could tell him the name of a cured Spanish ham. I said Serrano.

A mouse ran up the clock with a pork knuckle. It was a hickory dickory ham hock

Everyone else in Ms Fitzgerald's household had chocolate spread on their toast for breakfast. But Nutella.

I have a magic trick that makes a traditional Italian pine nut based sauce from straw. It's hay pesto.

Whenever I'm in my Spanish house, it is my duty to make the dinner in one dish. It's my casa role.

When I am cutting up cheese, I can never decide which of my knives to use. I end up using the one that is grater.

I always know when my Indian take away is delivered because I heard a chapatti door.

There was a large amount of Danish pastries, scones and cinnamon rolls at a disco. They were there in abundance.

I spilled a whole load of Bolognese on myself. I was covered from ma head tomato.

Have you heard about the injured rabbit beer? Barley hops.

MISCELLANEOUS

Whilst Ken jumped to the front of the line for his sausages and burgers, barbequed.

The cowboy insisted on using glue as a lubricant when everyone else disagreed. To be fair to him, he stuck to his guns.

A friend told me I should try this new drink but when he gave it to me it was a goblet with what smelled like fish. It was a poissoned chalice.

The other day I saw a tissue fondling a crumpet. It was just a bit of hanky pancake.

I wanted to put up a hedge to keep out intruders. I tried thorns- they were rubbish. I tried nettles- they were no good. So I tried drawing pins. Turns out a tack is the best thorn of de fence.

The tendency of a force to turn is something we need to torque about.

I went into a convent and asked how many people were there. I was told nun.

I fell in love with a glove. You could say I was smitten.

My girlfriend always nags me about the time I cheated on her with some linguine. She is always bringing up the pasta.

I created a book full of inspirational quotes and funny ideas on images that meant a lot to me personally. They were my memeoirs.

I spent all night wondering whether I should stay awake until the sun came up. Then it dawned on me.

Young voiceless chickens don't come cheap.

There was a story about a woman who had 3 sons all named Robert and she won the lottery. She wasn't short of a bob or two.

Someone asked me if I had a big enough van to help them move tomorrow. I said that no matter how big my van was, tomorrow would always be the day after today.

When I get my watch repaired, I'll occasionally go and visit my herb garden afterwards. I enjoy doing that from time to thyme.

I was tasked with creating a Monopoly board from scratch. Even though I don't know what to do with my first square, I think I'll make a go of it.

There is a tree that is absolutely obsessed with tactical board games. It is a chess nut. Apparently quite hard to conquer as well.

There was a bison, a fiesta car, and someone in a state of unconsciousness. That's called the Oxford coma.

A boat had lost its power but do you know how a brave warrior paddled them to shore? Hero.

The hallway didn't want to have its name changed to lobby but nobody could think of another alternative. But that's hallways foyer.

What did the giant say when he didn't want to pay a lot for an imitation mink coat? Fee high faux fur.

Did you know that the month of shock and surprise is nearly here? It's dismay.

The case of the missing unprocessed photos remains unsolved. I'll let you know if anything develops.

Our teacher asked us if anyone knew what the Latin word for year was. I said Anno.

The new intensive stitching class was sew sew.

A musician wrote and performed all his own songs dedicated to sewing machines. He was a singer songwriter.

I wanted to buy a feline from a Frenchman so I phoned him for a chat.

I made a mistake of trying to imitate 2 ghosts. It was a bit of a boo boo.

In splitting up your large lego bricks between your 2 children, you have to be duplomatic.

Breaking news! A farmer has ploughed only half of his field. More to fallow.

This girl once looked lovingly at me through donut spectacles. She was all doughy eyed.

Look at all those purply-blue colours entering that nightclub. Yeah, indigo.

I still measure in pounds and ounces but, when I go to Europe, I will change my weighs.

Did you hear about the tramp that was sounding off about nothing in particular? It was a vague rant.

My baby daughter was refusing to engage in buying her new crib and I'm not sure why. I think it was a boycott.

My friend Robert and I were going to have a toboggan race but didn't know whose would be the fastest but I would say bobs led.

I saw boxes of sandwiches, pasties and salads all tumbling down a mountain. It was an avalunch.

When I was in France, I was offered a dozen eggs for breakfast. I said, one egg is un eouf.

My mate insists that we only listen to electronic dance music. He won't techno for an answer.

I used this peasant slave to ride the waves. He was my serf board.

I don't know how i'm going to move this bed to my new house. Divan? Probably 'cos it looks too big for the car.

After fighting over who was going to get the ink pot first, I went in for the quill.

I was accused on hiding in a dollar bill but it couldn't have been me. I was in a cent.

Do you know why all the LGBT events in America take place before September? Because pride cometh before the fall.

You got to feel sorry for German cats. What with them having nein lives.

ABOUT THE AUTHOR

Iain lives in Glasgow, Scotland and produces daily content on Twitter, Tik Tok, Instagram and Facebook as well as having a YouTube channel featuring a lot of his comic content. All under the @imacpun username. He also does live shows around the country on a regular basis.

He also runs the UK Pun Off which has regular online shows as well as hosting the extensive back catalogue of shows. These can be found on YouTube and Facebook under the @ukpunoff username.

IAIN'S FINAL WORD

If you have made it this far then you might as well give me a follow on all of the above social media sites. If you enjoyed it, then there are always new jokes being written and posted daily and if you didn't enjoy it then maybe you can check it out to see if I have gotten any better! Thank you so much for buying this book. It has given me great satisfaction in being able to compile it and quite a bit of fun going through all the jokes that I have written over the years. Take care of yourselves and each other and I hope to see you someday. And if we do meet, ask me for a joke.

First printed edition October 2022
First audio edition October 2022

Book design by Iain MacDonald

ISBN 9798356484629

Printed in Great Britain
by Amazon

44587274R00079